19.95

NO WAY!

WACKY SPORTS

Michael J. Rosen

and Ben Kassoy

Illustrations by Doug Jones

M Millbrook Press • Minneapolis

Millbrook Press
A division of Lerner Publishing Group, Inc.
241 First Avenue North
Minneapolis, MN 55401 U.S.A.

Website address: www.lernerbooks.com

Main body text set in Adrianna Regular 12/16
Typeface provided by Chank

Rosen, Michael J., 1954–
    Wacky sports / by Michael J. Rosen and Ben Kassoy ; illustrations by Doug Jones.
        p.   cm.
    Includes index.
    ISBN 978-0-7613-8982-8 (lib. bdg. : alk. paper)
    ISBN 978-1-4677-1708-3 (eBook)
    1. Sports—Juvenile literature. 2. Entertainment—Juvenile literature.
I. Kassoy, Ben. II. Jones, Doug, 1950– illustrator. III. Title.
GV704.5.R67 2014
796—dc23   2012048933

Manufactured in the United States of America
1 – BP – 7/15/13

The authors would like to recognize the generous contribution of Christoffer Strömstedt, as well as the efforts of Ashley Heestand, Colin Stoecker, and Claire Hamilton in the researching, fact-checking, and drafting of the No Way! series of books.

The images in this book are used with the permission of: © Stephanie Fysh/Flickr Select/Getty Images, p. 4; Alexandra Beier/Reuters/Newscom, p. 5; REUTERS/Lucas Jackson, p. 6; © Frans Lemmens/Alamy, p. 9; Minneapolis Star Tribune/Zuma Press/Newscom, p. 11 (top); Jeremy Young/Rex USA, p. 11 (bottom); Courtesy of The Kiiking Community, p. 13; © Heikki Saukkomma/Stringer/Getty Images, p. 14; © Matthew Lloyd/Stringer/Getty Images, p. 16; Wolfgang Kumm/EPA/Newscom, p. 17; © Udo Weitz/EPA/CORBIS, p. 18; © Andy Sewell/VisitBritain/Britain On View/Getty Images, p. 21 (top); © Jeff Morgan 10/Alamy, p. 21 (bottom); © Matt Cardy/Stringer/Getty Images, p. 23 (top); Splash News/Newscom, p. 23 (bottom); © Visited Planet , p. 25 (all); © Emma Wood/Britain On View/Getty Images, p. 27 (top); © Terje Eggum/AFP/Getty Images, p. 27 (bottom); © Jonnathan Colt Photography/San Francisco, p. 29.
Front cover: © Visited Planet.

TABLE of CONTENTS

NOT JUST SPLASHING AROUND • SPLASHDIVING ... 4

KNOCKING YOUR LIGHTS OUT • PILLOW FIGHTING ... 6

UP, UP AND AWAY • DITCH VAULTING ... 8

TAKE THE PLUNGE • OCTOPUSH ... 10

SET YOUR SIGHTS ON THIS SWING SET • KIIKING ... 12

BALLS AWAY • YUKIGASSEN ... 14

CHECKMATE ... KNOCKOUT! • CHESS BOXING ... 16

SUPERSIZE ME • ELEPHANT POLO ... 18

BOGGED DOWN • BOG SNORKELING ... 20

WHEELS OF MISFORTUNE • CHEESE ROLLING ... 22

IT'S A SKI-FOR-ALL • WATERMELON SKIING ... 24

KEEPING YOUR COOL • EXREME COLD WATER SWIMMING ... 26

ON A ROLL • ROLLERSOCCER ... 28

Glossary ... 30

Source Notes ... 31

Further Reading ... 31

Index ... 32

NOT JUST SPLASHING AROUND
SPLASHDIVING

Have you ever done a belly flop off the diving board? Ever challenged your buddies to a cannonball contest? Wanted to see who made the biggest splash? Now would you ever think those games could be an actual sport?

Splashdiving was "invented" in Germany. But everyone knows the basic idea. The person who makes the highest and widest sprays of water wins. In the official sport, a panel of judges rates each jump based on execution (how well it's done) and degree of difficulty.

Divers are ranked by skill. You start as a hopper. After mastering the moves at that level, you rise to jumper. Then diver. Then master. Then champion. Go all the way, and you could reach the top rank: baron.

Splashdivers can choose from a whole range of potentially painful jumps!

This watery punishment is gaining popularity. The sport has fans all over Europe, Australia, and the Philippines. The language of skin smacking water must be universal!

There are even junior events for kids. (Can you picture your parents' thrilled faces?) Yes, this sport is open to anyone daring enough to take the plunge. According to the official website, "Splashdiving is . . . a community for girls, boys, and especially freaks."

KNOCKING YOUR LIGHTS OUT

PILLOW FIGHTING

Isn't pillow fighting just for sleepover parties? Sorry, but times have changed! Welcome to the Pillow Fight World Cup. At this event, uniformed opponents bash it out in front of cheering crowds. Pajamas not allowed.

Contenders from Europe, Asia, and the United States compete in this wacky event. "It's less brutal than boxing," admitted one competitor. "But you still need technique."

An Austrian competitor *(left)* aims for an American pillow fighter during the Pillow Fight World Cup.

Once inside the ring, fighters fling their fluffy weapons—*fwawp!* Judges award points for shots to the head or body. *Shwoop!* They deduct points if a competitor touches the mat with the pillow or a hand. *Moof!* A blow that lands an opponent on both knees is considered a knockout.

The World Cup is just for women. But foes of both sexes, armed with feathered weapons, compete in various events from Canada to Austria to Indonesia. They may fight while sitting astride a slippery pole. They might battle onstage next to a punk band. They may fight one-on-one. Or it could be a ten-person battle royal. However the matches are staged, after all that action, fighters are tired enough for a nap. Good thing they already have pillows, huh?

UP, UP AND AWAY
DITCH VAULTING

Fierljeppen [FEERL-YEP-uhn], which is Dutch for "far leaping," is a one-of-a-kind climbing sport. It started in Holland, a part of the Netherlands. English speakers call the sport ditch vaulting. Sane people call it crazy.

The sport requires a dock, a small canal, a 43-foot-long (13-meter) pole, and a pit of sand. Oh, and also athletes with the climbing skills of a monkey.

So what's the event? You, the ditch vaulter, sprint down the long dock. You grab the pole that's anchored in the canal. You shinny up the pole as high as possible as it falls toward the other bank. Before the pole hits the shore, you jump, springing into the sandpit. Whoever lands farthest away from the start wins.

Ditch vaulters in action in the Netherlands.

This daring sport began as sort of transportation. As early as the year 1200, the Dutch used poles to vault across the many waterways that divided plots of land in Holland. The first organized competition was arranged in 1771. *Game on!*

This sport isn't child's play—even if kids and teenagers can compete in the sixteen-and-under division. The world record is 70.57 feet (21.51 m). That's long enough to sail over a fin whale—second only to the blue whale in size—should one happen to be swimming in the canal.

TAKE THE PLUNGE
OCTOPUSH

Close your eyes and imagine an ice hockey game. Now imagine all the ice has melted. Next, substitute swim fins for the skates. Replace the helmets with masks and snorkels. Okay! Now you're ready for underwater hockey!

Also known as octopush, this sport pits two six-member teams against one another in an underwater "rink." Each player carries a stick that's about 1 foot (0.3 m) long. Players use the sticks to pass and shoot a 3-pound (1.36-kilogram) puck, nicknamed a squid. The heavy puck sinks, so the game is played along the bottom of the pool. Any player that carries or bounces the puck receives a penalty. Bet you never thought you'd hear a referee shout, "No dribbling the squid!"

This wet and wild battle takes place entirely underwater. But a player can't play the entire game on one breath. So the action includes a quick rise to the surface, a gulp of air, and a dive back into the game. The best octopush players have big lung capacity. And the speed and agility of a dolphin ... a stick-carrying dolphin, that is.

Just as in ice hockey, the action in octopush is fast, furious, and physical. The two sports share one other feature: plenty of *ouches!*

SET YOUR SIGHTS ON THIS SWING SET
KiiKiNG

On playground swings, higher is definitely more fun. But swing too high—or worse, stand up on a swing—and you'll get the whistle blown at you.

Not so, in the sport of *kiiking* [KEE-kihng]. Too high doesn't exist. In fact, swinging over the bar is the only way to win!

Created in the eastern European country of Estonia, kiiking comes from *kiik* [KEEK]. This Estonian word means "swing." For centuries, people rode giant wooden swings at village festivals. But competitive kiiking is a new form of nuttiness!

The kiiking swing has tubular metal arms instead of ropes or chains. The arms lengthen every round to make the action more difficult, stretching from about 10 feet (3 m) to 26 feet (8 m). The longer the arms, the harder it is to swing over the bar.

Breaking all playground rules you know, competitors *must* stand up. Their hands and feet are strapped to the swing. To get the heavy swing moving, competitors pump their whole bodies. They bend their knees. They squat down. They thrust their bodies forward and backward. Competitors say you don't really start *kiiking* until your legs are above your head!

Each swinger has five minutes to complete one circle over the bar. But few contenders have the leg muscles or staying power to last even three minutes. The winner is the one who completes a full circle on the swing with the longest arms. The world record is just over 23 feet (7 m). The U.S. record is about 17 feet (5 m).

If only you could practice your *kiiking* during recess. You could be the next champion!

BALLS AWAY
YUKIGASSEN

In your neighborhood, snowball fighting may be a winter pastime. In Japan it's become a competitive team sport known as yukigassen [yoo-kee-GAH-sehn]! The world championships take place atop a volcano. Even if the volcano is inactive—*phew!*—the action is totally explosive.

Each game consists of three, three-minute rounds. Seven-member teams are allotted ninety perfectly shaped snowballs per round. Then . . . *throw* get 'em!

Like hockey players, competitors wear shielded masks. Like secret agents, they duck, dive, and dodge behind frozen barricades to avoid getting hit. And the goal? Capture your opponents' flag or wipe them all out with your chilly artillery.

A competitor takes aim at the 2010 Finnish yukigassen championships.

So, who makes all those snowballs? Not who but *what*. It's the official "dumpling-style" snowball maker! It's similar to an ice tray but with rounded slots. Fill it with moist snow, close the rounded lid, knock off the extra snow . . . and, *presto!* a tray of regulation snowballs.

Yukigassen isn't just a Japanese phenomenon. Countries across Asia, Europe, and North America host their own tournaments and send teams to international competitions. Some U.S. competitions offer a high-school division. Maybe in a few years, you can take your snowball-firing skills from the backyard to the big stage!

CHECKMATE... KNOCKOUT!
CHESS BOXING

Picture a chess player: someone who is really smart and probably not too strong. Picture a boxer: a lean, mean, punching machine with a brain that might be on the blink from being bonked so many times.

Now picture the two as one. What have you got? A chess boxer! It's the ultimate balance of brains and brawn. Someone mentally nimble on the checkered board and physically nimble in the squared circle.

Chess boxing's slogan could be "Bring your brain . . . but prepare for pain!"

Men—and, since 2011, women—compete in World Chess Boxing Organisation matches. Each match starts with speed chess. Opponents move their chessmen under the pressure of the clock. Four minutes later . . . *ding!* The fighters have one minute to trade their kings and knights for gloves and mouth guards. *Ding!* Now it's three minutes to punch it out. *Ding!* Back to the chessboard.

Bouts alternate (up to six rounds of chess and five rounds of boxing) until there's a winner. Victory can come in the ring: *knockout!* It can come on the chessboard: *checkmate!* Players can also win by racking up the most points or by disqualification.

An elementary school in Germany even includes chess boxing in its gym classes! Maybe it's time to ask your gym teacher if you can try "the thinking man's contact sport."

SUPERSIZE ME
ELEPHANT POLO

The British have ridden horses in games of polo for more than one hundred years. In the "old-fashioned" version, riders pass or shoot a ball into a goal by using long wooden mallets.

Polo actually began halfway around the world, in Asia—most likely Persia. In recent years, the Asian countries of Nepal and Thailand have put a new twist on the game. It's become supersized! The new version of the game is elephant polo.

In this humongous adaptation, players perch upon pachyderms. To reach the ground, mallets have grown too. They are about 6.5 feet (2 m) long, which is taller than most full-grown men! Players compete in pairs. The mahout—the elephant's trainer and caretaker—steers the elephant. The other player holds the mallet. That person moves, passes, and attempts to shoot the ball into the goal.

Rain and mud were no obstacle for these players at a match in Thailand.

It's easier said than done! Look at all these potential problems:

• Elephants can block the players' sight of the ball. Instead of cheering, fans yell out its location. "*It's under the elephant! No, the other elephant!*"

• An elephant can block the goal by lying down in front of it. Smart defense? Nope. In fact, it's an illegal move.

• An elephant can decide to pick up the ball with its trunk. (That's also against the rules.)

• Dung! Elephants eat tons of food every day . . . and what goes in has to come out. Good thing the players are high off the ground.

BOGGED DOWN
BOG SNORKELING

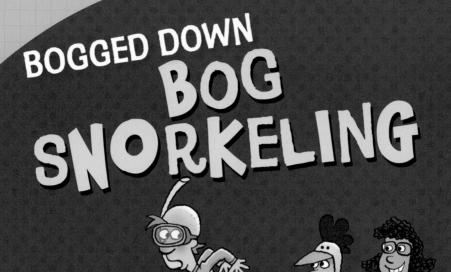

Would you take a bath in a mud puddle? Of course not—unless you're in Wales, United Kingdom, during the World Bog Snorkelling Championships. People swim in what's been described as "bug-infested soup."

The only thing harder than pronouncing Waen Rhydd Bog [WEYEN RUHD BAHG] is swimming in it. Competitors must dog paddle (that's the only legal stroke). And the water's so thick the swimmers can barely see as they slap, slop, and splash through 60 yards (55 m) of slime, weeds, and muck.

Beyond the standard uniform of a snorkel and flippers, serious competitors wear wet suits. Some of the sillier swimmers show up in costume. One competitor even wore footie pajamas! But bog swimming is hardly something you can do in your sleep. Most competitors admit it's a lot harder than it looks.

A bog snorkeler needs a snorkel, a mask, and the courage to jump in the muck!

Still, some make it look easy. Recent winners are making the swim in record times of less than ninety seconds!

The younger cousin of bog snorkeling is the World Mountain Bike Bog Snorkelling Championships. Competitors fill their bike frames with small lead pellets to make them sink. Then they zoom through the muck. The one rule: keep the water at eye level the entire time.

But why stop there? The bog triathlon adds one more event to this downright dirty ordeal. Athletes run 7.5 miles (12 kilometers), swim two lengths of the bog, and then hop back out and bike for 19 miles (31 km). Talk about feeling bogged down!

WHEELS OF MISFORTUNE
CHEESE ROLLING

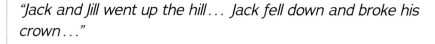

"Jack and Jill went up the hill . . . Jack fell down and broke his crown . . ."

Hold on! Is it possible that this age-old nursery rhyme describes the sport of cheese rolling?

Every year, dozens of otherwise sensible citizens stand at the crest of Cooper's Hill. It's an extremely steep slope in Gloucester [GLOW-stihr], United Kingdom. Suddenly, a 7-or 8-pound (3 or 3.6 kg) wheel of Double Gloucester cheese is thrown down the hill. Why cheese? Why would you ask "why" if the competitors don't? They run, slide, and tumble as they chase after it. The first one to the bottom—typically arriving on his or her bottom—is the winner.

The cheese wheel zooms down the steep slope of Cooper's Hill at up to 70 miles (112 km) per hour. That's as fast as a car on the freeway! In fact, it's so fast that local law classifies the cheese as a *missile*.

The competitors also bound and bounce with uncontrollable speed down the hill. As a safety measure, local rugby players line up at the bottom of the hill to halt the grass-stained cheese chasers. Can you imagine a rugby player's tackle "softening" your fall?

Local officials have tried to ban the competition because of injuries. But the two-hundred-year-old tradition continues. People just can't wait to conquer Cooper's Hill.

So what's the prize? The winner takes the cheese!

Jemima Bullock came all the way from New Zealand to win the women's race—and the cheese!

IT'S A SKI-FOR-ALL
WATERMELON SKIING

Ah, the sounds of waterskiing! The *vroom* of the motorboat! The *shush* of the skis skidding across the water! The *smack* of a well-earned tumble!

What you won't hear while skiing is a *squish*—unless you visit Chinchilla. It's the Melon Capital of Australia. Every two years, this town of thirty-six hundred hosts Melonfest. Melonfest features the famous, super-silly event of melon skiing.

The only water needed for this kind of skiing is watermelons! Competitors stick their feet inside hollowed melons. They grab hold of a towrope. Then they try to balance as pullers yank them down a 164-foot (50 m) course. The course itself is a slippery slide. It's a plastic tarp covered with soapsuds and melon guts.

Wearing seedy skis is only part of the challenge in this slippery sport!

You'll also hear one more sound in melon skiing: *splat!* That's the crash of another skier being flung from that fruity footwear.

Melonfest offers other mushy matches for the ten thousand visitors. Melon bull's-eye is a bit like darts. But you heave *watermelons* at the target.

If you really want to use your head, sign up for melon smashing. The object of this event? Crack as many melons as possible using your own melon! Can you split open forty-eight watermelons in a minute? The Guinness World Record could be yours.

KEEPING YOUR COOL
EXREME COLD WATER SWIMMING

Water freezes at 32°F (0°C). Extreme cold water swimming events take place in water as close to that freezing point as possible. Any colder and participants would be backstroking through a pool-sized snow cone.

How do you handle such an icy race? Maybe you dip in your toe to test the temperature. You get up your courage. You just—you just—okay! *You plunge in!* A second later, popping to the surface, you shout, *"Yikes! It's SO freezing!"* But in water this frigid, a headfirst dive can knock out a swimmer—cold!

Even conditions *outside* the pool are hazardous. At your pool, the rule may be no running on the deck. At these events, it's so cold that competitors are told not to even walk barefoot.

Surprisingly, some extreme cold water swimmers claim the sport has benefits beyond cheers from the crowd. They say dipping your body in water suited for polar bears boosts your immune system, improves circulation, and burns tons of extra calories.

Still, no one can stay in such frosty conditions for long. As one veteran swimmer puts it, when you have a "miserable, aching cold deep inside you. That's probably a good time to get out."

As if there were a *good* time to get *in*.

Lewis Gordon Pugh is famous for his cold water swimming adventures.

ON A ROLL
ROLLERSOCCER

Love soccer? Love rollerblading? Then put the two together! That's what Zack Phillips did when he created RollerSoccer.

Players skate up and down a roller hockey rink. But they dribble, pass, and shoot a soccer ball. No hands, of course! Not even a goalie's! (In most games, there are no goalies.) And games are so fast-paced that players wipe out often.

On offense, players can choose from three different kicks. The side kick uses the inside of a skate for an accurate, controlled blow. A toe kick provides shooting power. Skilled players can use the difficult instep kick for both accuracy and power. They strike the ball toward the goal with the top outside of a skate.

Zack Phillips created RollerSoccer in San Francisco, California, in 1995, and it caught on fast. The RollerSoccer World Cup has become so popular that it's an annual event.

Try it! You might get a kick out of it! Or consider these two other soccer variations.

Hate grass stains? Try swamp soccer! It's played on a flooded, muddy field. Just sloshing from one goal to the other is even more difficult than scoring.

Or try snow soccer. You'll need heavy boots for crossing the snow and padded pants to protect you from the sting of a frozen ball. And don't forget your scarf! Do you want to catch a cold?

GLOSSARY

artillery: any sort of weapon used in combats or competitions

battle royal: a fight among a small or large group of people. Typically, the winner is the last person left standing.

bog: ground that is wet or underwater, composed of mostly rotted vegetation

bout: one of the short periods of action that make up a boxing or wrestling match

century: a period of exactly one hundred years

disqualification: the removal of a person or team from a competition because of a broken rule or a failure to meet the required standards

dung: an animal's poop

endure: to fight through pain or exhaustion or hardship

execution: performing a maneuver or carrying out a play

fling: throw forcefully

immune system: the body's natural defenses against disease or infection

knockout: in boxing, a knockout is declared when a competitor is punched, falls to the mat, and cannot stand before the referee counts to a certain number

lung capacity: the amount of air a person—inhaling as deeply as possible—can hold in the lungs

mahout: someone who cares for, trains, and "drives" an elephant, riding at the animal's neck

missile: an object zooming through the air

offense: actions and plays that attempt to score

on the blink: currently not working

pachyderm: a hooved, thick-skinned mammal such as an elephant, hippopotamus, or rhinoceros

plummet: fall quickly downward

precaution: a careful action taken in the hope of preventing future trouble

rugby: a fast-paced sport that's something like a combination of football and soccer. Two fifteen-member teams may tackle opponents, kick the ball, or use their hands to block or carry the oval-shaped ball.

sane: mentally capable

shinny: scramble up a pole

snorkel: a tube, usually attached to a mask, that allows a swimmer to breathe underwater

squared circle: a square space, usually surrounded by ropes, in which competitors box or wrestle

triathlon: a race in which competitors swim, run, and bicycle

tubular: shaped like a tube or pipe

yogi: a person who practices yoga

SOURCE NOTES

5   "Jump Up, Move It and Splash Down," n.d., Splashdiving International, http://www.splashdiving.com/index .php?ida=120&L=3 (July 27, 2012).

6   Michael McLaughlin, "Pillow Fight World Cup Ruffles Fine Feathered Foes," May 17, 2011, http://www .huffingtonpost.com/2011/05/17/pillow-fight-world-cup-ru_n_862789.html (July 27, 2012).

17 Chessboxing, n.d., http://www.chessboxing.com (July 27, 2012).

20 "Exposed on Channel 7 News, the Week Ender, Sunrise & Soon to Be Kerri-Anne!" February 10, 2005, http://www.bogsnorkelling.com/press.htm (July 27, 2012).

27 Andrew Berg, "What It Takes: Lewis Gordon Pugh," n.d., http://www.nationalgeographic.com /adventure/0605/whats_new/lewis_gordon_pugh.html (July 27, 2012).

FURTHER READING

BOOKS

Berman, Len. *And Nobody Got Hurt!: The World's Weirdest, Wackiest True Sports Stories.* New York: Little, Brown and Company, 2005.
Even normal, everyday sports like baseball, basketball, and tennis have weird things happen every once in a while, and this book highlights the best of them.

Crossingham, John, and Bobbie Kalman. *Extreme Sports.* New York: Crabtree Pub. Co., 2004.
This book offers a survey of the stranger and more risky competitions that athletes undertake. It also includes profiles of these thrill-seekers.

Kelley, K. C. *Weird Races*. Weird Sports. Chanhassen, MN: Child's World, 2011.
Weird Races covers the world's strangest racing competitions. Ever heard about ostrich racing or toilet racing? Well, you can learn all about them here.

Smith, Penny. *To the Extreme: Dangerous Sports and Daredevil Jobs.* New York: DK Publishing, 2011.
This book takes an inside look at the most extreme things people do for fun and for money. Learn how people explore caves, fight forest fires, collect snake venom, and more.

WEBSITES

KIDS WORLD SPORTS

http://pbskids.org/kws/

This site features short profiles of many sports, as well as profiles of young, up-and-coming athletes.

Each of the sports featured in the book has its own website. Most feature current events, photographs, videos, official rules, profiles of competitors, and much more. While they're not written for kids, you'll still find plenty of valuable and amusing information.

BOG SNORKELING
http://www.bogsnorkelling.com

CHEESE ROLLING
http://www.cheese-rolling.co.uk

CHESS BOXING
http://www.wcbo.org

DITCH VAULTING
http://www.pbholland.com/?&lang=en

ELEPHANT POLO
http://www.elephantpolo.com

EXTREME COLD WATER SWIMMING
http://www.slsc.org.uk

KIIKING
http://www.kiiking.ee

OCTOPUSH
http://www.usauwh.com

PILLOW FIGHTING
http://www.pillowfightworldcup.com

ROLLER SOCCER
http://www.RollerSoccer.com

SPLASHDIVING
http://www.splashdiving.com

WATERMELON SKIING
http://www.melonfest.com.au/index-tess1.php?ItemNo=1004&site=375

YUKIGASSEN
http://www.yukigassen.jp

INDEX

Asia, 6, 15, 18
Australia, 5
Austria, 7

bog snorkeling, 20–21

Canada, 7
cheese rolling, 22–23
chess boxing, 16–17
Chinchilla, Australia, 24
cold water swimming, 26–27
competitive swinging, 12–13

ditch vaulting, 8–9

elephant polo, 18–19
Estonia, 12

Europe, 5, 6, 15

Germany, 4, 17
Gloucester, United Kingdom, 22

Indonesia, 7

Japan, 14

kiiking, 12–13

Nepal, 18
Netherlands, 8
North America, 15

octopush, 10–11

Persia, 18

Philippines, 5
pillow fighting, 6–7
RollerSoccer, 28–29

San Francisco, California, 29
snowball fighting, 14–15
splashdiving, 4–5

Thailand, 18

underwater hockey, 10–11
United States, 6

Wales, United Kingdom, 20
watermelon skiing, 24–25

Yukigassen, 14–15